Selling More Snacks

Vickie An

Contributing Author

Heather Schultz, M.A.

Consultants

Ashley R. Young, Ph.D.
Historian
National Museum of American History

Tamieka Grizzle, Ed.D.
K–5 STEM Lab Instructor
Harmony Leland Elementary School

Stephanie Anastasopoulos, M.Ed.
TOSA, STREAM Integration
Solana Beach School District

Publishing Credits

Rachelle Cracchiolo, M.S.Ed., *Publisher*
Conni Medina, M.A.Ed., *Managing Editor*
Diana Kenney, M.A.Ed., NBCT, *Series Developer*
June Kikuchi, *Content Director*
Véronique Bos, *Creative Director*
Robin Erickson, *Art Director*
Seth Rogers, *Editor*
Mindy Duits, *Senior Graphic Designer*
Smithsonian Science Education Center

Image Credits: p.5 (top) National News/Zuma Press/Newscom; p.7 (top) Don Mammoser/Alamy; p.8 (insert) Getty Images; p.10 (bottom) Agricultural Research Service/U.S. Department of Agriculture/Science Source; p.11 (top) Robert Landau/Alamy; p.15 (bottom) 06photo/ Shutterstock; p.19 Radu Bercan/Shutterstock; p.20 (bottom) Jeff Miller/ University of Wisconsin-Madison; p.27 Reuters/Gleb Bryanski; all other images from iStock and/or Shutterstock.

Library of Congress Cataloging-in-Publication Data

Names: An, Vickie, author.
Title: Selling more snacks / Vickie An.
Description: Huntington Beach, CA : Teacher Created Materials, [2019] | Includes index. |
Identifiers: LCCN 2018005247 (print) | LCCN 2018017767 (ebook) | ISBN 9781493869398 (E-book) | ISBN 9781493866991 (pbk.)
Subjects: LCSH: Snack foods--Juvenile literature. | Snack food industry--Juvenile literature.
Classification: LCC TX370 (ebook) | LCC TX370 .A524 2019 (print) | DDC 641.5/3--dc23
LC record available at https://lccn.loc.gov/2018005247

Smithsonian

Teacher Created Materials

5301 Oceanus Drive
Huntington Beach, CA 92649-1030
www.tcmpub.com

ISBN 978-1-4938-6699-1

Table of Contents

Nation of Snackers

You come home from school and your stomach is rumbling. "Feed me!" it growls. So you stroll into the kitchen to find a snack. What do you usually reach for? Do you grab a granola bar? How about a bag of cheddar cheese crackers? Or maybe some fresh baby carrots? Whatever you choose, you have many options. That is because snacks are easier to come across than ever before.

Snacking has become a regular part of the day for many people. From popcorn and apples to yogurt and ice cream, take a trip to any grocery store and you will find all kinds of delicious treats in the aisles. These foods and more became popular in the 1950s snack **revolution**. Since then, **innovations** (ih-nuh-VAY-shunz) in food have made snacks much easier to munch on the go. And there are more choices than ever before.

The world's biggest bag of potato chips weighed more than 1,140 kilogram (2,515 pounds). That is as much as a small car!

Snacking through the Years

Some snacks people eat today have been around for a long time. Popcorn and pretzels are two of the world's oldest snack foods. But which one came first? Historians aren't sure. Some say popcorn came first. The airy snack comes from a type of corn plant. It dates back thousands of years. One of the oldest popped corncobs was found in Peru, a country in South America. Back then people roasted the cobs over fire until the kernels popped.

What's Poppin'?

Popcorn got a popularity boost in the mid-1800s. That is when the planting of corn became widespread in the United States. People liked the fluffy snack because it was tasty and cheap. Over the years, they enjoyed it at fairs, in parks, and in movie theaters. The invention of microwave popcorn in the 1980s made it even easier for people to make it at home.

A man makes popcorn at a market in India.

MATHEMATICS

Pop Secret

Most of the world's corn that is used for popcorn is grown in the United States. But popcorn is enjoyed all over the world. Each kernel has a hard outer shell called a **hull**. There is a small drop of water inside each hull that is surrounded by **starch**. Most corn kernels pop when the temperature inside reaches 200°–240° Celsius (400°–460° Fahrenheit). The water turns to steam. Pressure from the steam builds until the hull finally bursts and turns inside out.

One Twisted Snack

Pretzels have a long history, too. But no one knows for sure who made the first pretzel. One **legend** says Italian **monks** first made the soft snack about 1,500 years ago. The monks twisted dough to look like arms crossed in prayer. They used the baked goods to reward their students. Some people say the word *pretzel* comes from the Latin word *pretiola*. It means "little reward."

Hard pretzels were first made in the United States in 1861. The history of this snack is filled with legends as well. Some people say that Julius Sturgis was making soft pretzels at his bakery in Pennsylvania. One batch of pretzels was left in the oven for too long and burned. Sturgis tried them anyway. He thought they were crisp and tasty. Other people say that hard pretzels were made on purpose because they would last a lot longer than soft pretzels. Either way, the hard pretzel was born!

A 15th century baker sells pretzels.

Baker Helen Hoff holds the world record for pretzel twisting. She can twist 57 pretzels in one minute!

ENGINEERING

Preparing Pretzels

Most pretzels are made by machines. First, about 50 kg (110 lb.) of dough is placed on a **conveyor belt**. Machines roll and cut the dough to the right thickness and length. Then, a "twister" machine shapes the dough. Machines drop the pretzels into liquid and then salt them. Finally, machines transfer the pretzels to ovens, then to be dried and packaged.

The Science of Food

Hard pretzels were the result of a mistake. But today, there are workers whose only job is to think of new food products. Part of that job involves finding ways to make food tastier and longer-lasting. These people work in food science.

Food science is the study of food. Food scientists get paid to play with their food. It is their job to make the foods we love even better. To do so, they test different products at food and drink companies and research new ingredients in labs. They also work to make sure food is safe to eat. Their work includes many people's favorite packaged snacks.

Food for Thought

Food scientists use scientific practices to help them make foods better. They ask questions to define the problems. Then, they plan and carry out investigations. They analyze and interpret data. Food scientists use this data to design solutions for problems.

A food scientist works on a low-fat cheese.

SCIENCE

Quick, Easy, and Cheesy

In the 1950s, food scientists at Kraft® were asked to create a packaged cheese sauce that would save people time in the kitchen. The sauce had to stay soft. It had to melt well when heated. And it had to last a long time. They mixed different cheeses with food coloring, salts, and **emulsifiers**, which kept the liquids from separating. They spent more than a year experimenting. The result was Cheez Whiz®.

Food scientists have many problems to solve. They may ask how they can make ice cream creamier. Or, what kind of packaging will keep fruit fresh the longest. Some food scientists want to know how to make potato chips taste like a hamburger. Or, how they can remove fat from food without changing its taste. Food scientists spend their days solving these types of problems.

Extra, Extra!

Food scientists sometimes work with **additives**. These are natural or manmade ingredients that are added to food. The use of additives began rising in the 1950s. Companies still use them today to try to change products. They can make foods taste better. They can change the color and texture of food. Additives can also keep food fresh longer.

Some ice cream has additives to make it creamier.

It takes 45 kg (100 lb.) of potatoes to make 11 kg (25 lb.) of chips!

The number of snack choices has soared in the last 70 years. The invention of additives and new food technologies have helped. Today, food companies make snacks in all shapes, sizes, and flavors. Do you **crave** something salty? Try some roasted nuts. You can even eat crackers that taste like pizza. Do you have a sweet tooth? Hundreds of options line supermarket shelves!

You Are What You Eat

There is a downside to all this snacking, though. People believe that the popularity of junk food has led to less healthy eating habits. Doctors worry it is causing a rise in childhood **obesity**. So, how can packaged snacks be healthier? That is one more question for food scientists to answer.

One solution is to create recipes that lower the amounts of fat, salt, and sugar found in snack foods and drinks. But how do you keep flavors the same? It is tough!

Supermarket aisles are packed with both healthy and unhealthy snacking options.

Some healthy snacks also have additives. You have most likely seen diet soda and sugar-free candy at supermarkets. Scientists have taken the sugar out of these products. They have replaced it with fake sweeteners. These make food and drinks sweet without adding calories.

The Skinny on Calories

A *calorie* is a unit of measurement. It tells you how much energy your body could get from eating something. Most food and drinks have calories. Some have more than others. Bodies need calories for energy. They help keep people moving. Kids need calories to grow, too.

Eating more calories than you use can lead to weight gain. This is especially true if you do not use them by playing and exercising. Gaining too much weight can cause health problems. That's why it is important to make good food choices.

Nutrition Facts

Serving Size 2 oz (56g - about 1/7 box)
Servings Per Container about 7

Amount Per Serving

Calories 200

	% Daily Value*
Total Fat 6.5g	2%
Saturated Fat 4g	0%
Trans Fat 2g	
Cholesterol 0mg	0%
Sodium 10mg	0%
Total Carbohydrate 41g	14%
Dietary Fiber 6g	24%
Sugars 2g	
Protein 7g	

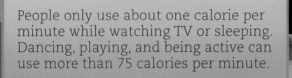

People only use about one calorie per minute while watching TV or sleeping. Dancing, playing, and being active can use more than 75 calories per minute.

Using Your Senses

A lot of times, people use all five senses when choosing foods to eat. That's right. Eating is not just about how food tastes. It is about seeing food, smelling food, touching food, and even listening to food. Food scientists keep all these things in mind when they create and test recipes.

Our eyes are the first things we use when we eat. Imagine you are in your kitchen looking for a snack. You grab a strawberry yogurt from the refrigerator and peel off the top. What is the first thing you notice? The pink color, right? But this color may not come from the strawberries in it. Sometimes, scientists use food dyes to make yogurt pink. They do this to **enhance** appearance. In this case, food coloring might trick your brain into thinking the yogurt tastes more like strawberries than it really does.

Colorful Cues

Chip designers use specific colors in packaging to match certain flavors. Sour cream and onion chips commonly come in green bags. This is so shoppers will think of green onions. Bags of barbecue chips usually come in deep red bags, just like barbecue sauce. These color **cues** make it easier for shoppers to identify flavors quickly.

19

Natural and **artificial** scents and flavoring might also be added. After all, the better something smells, the more appealing it is and the more someone will want to try it!

Food scientists might also try to make textures of foods more pleasing. One example of this is a special ingredient that is added to ice cream. It helps keep ice crystals from forming. It also keeps the frozen food creamy.

That covers four of the five senses, but what about sound? How do people use their ears to eat? Just listen. Listen to the crisp crunch of an apple as you take a bite. Listen to the crackling sound of cereal as you pour milk into your bowl. Senses all play a part as people eat food.

In 2015, a group of University of Wisconsin students set a record. They made a record-breaking Rice Krispies® treat that weighed 5,138 kg (11,327 lb.).

The sounds of food cooking or being eaten can make people hungry.

Think Fast

Families stay busy these days. Many parents work all day, and kids are busy with activities after school. Food companies know that to sell their products they have to make foods that are cheap and **convenient** (kuhn-VEEN-yuhnt). Modern factories and food processing let them do just that.

Fresh foods, such as meats, vegetables, and fruits, can go bad quickly. So, scientists have come up with ways to preserve food, making it last longer. This is known as food processing. Foods that have been processed often contain additives. All packaged snack foods, from string cheese to beef jerky, have been processed. Those baby carrots you chomp on? Those are processed, too. Even though they are vegetables, they still get peeled and cleaned in a factory. Then, they are sorted and sealed in plastic bags, ready to eat.

Carrots are peeled and cleaned to make baby carrots.

Keeping It Fresh

People have been finding ways to preserve food for thousands of years. Before there were freezers and refrigerators, people had to develop ways to make food, such as meat, last longer. They learned that they could keep meat for long periods of time by rubbing the meat in salt, spices, and other ingredients before hanging it to dry. This is called **curing**. It is a common practice today.

Factories have made it easier to process foods, too. Companies hire teams of engineers to design machines and tools that meet their needs. The equipment allows them to prepare, create, and package a lot of food quickly. This saves companies time and money. As a result, customers save time, too. Think about your favorite snacks. How many do you think are processed?

Many people expect to be able to buy their favorite snacks anytime they want. This has led to a rise in convenience stores. These corner shops have been a popular stop for snacks and beverages since the mid-1900s. The stores are just what their names say. They make it easy for customers to grab a snack and go. They are found almost everywhere. They are open for long hours. And they can often be closer than the nearest grocery store.

This type of cash register might have been used in a general store.

FIVE & DIME
GENERAL STORE

Where did the convenience store 7-Eleven® get its name? The store used to be open from 7:00 a.m. to 11:00 p.m.

This machine quickly gets dumplings ready to package.

Chew on This

Snacks that can be eaten on the run are a big part of today's eating habits. Innovations in the food industry have made it easier to snack anywhere and everywhere. People snack at home. Kids snack at school. Adults snack at work. With drive-thru windows, people do not even need to leave their cars to buy snacks. Food companies are always challenging their food scientists to come up with products to sell in quick and convenient ways.

But that speed and convenience has led to more unhealthy eating habits. It is all about the choices you make. If you choose more healthy foods, snacks can still be part of a balanced diet. So, what will you reach for today?

A "ski-thru" opened in Sweden in 1996.

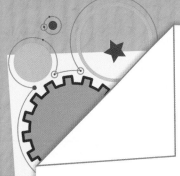

STEAM CHALLENGE

Define the Problem

A food scientist has asked you to help create a delicious snack for kids. Use what you have learned about snacks to make 170 grams (6 ounces) of a snack mix to use as a sample.

Constraints: Your sample snack mix must be under 300 calories. The snack mix must contain at least three different ingredients.

Criteria: The snack mix must be taste-tested and approved by at least five kids. (**Note:** Give your testers a list of ingredients to make sure they are not allergic to anything in your recipe.)

Research and Brainstorm

What should you consider when making a snack healthier? Will you focus on calories or taste first? How does your target customer change your recipe?

Design and Build

List your ingredients and their calorie counts. How much of each ingredient will you use to create your mix? Include how much of each ingredient is needed to create 170 g (6 oz.) of your recipe. Combine ingredients to create your snack.

Test and Improve

Ask your testers to judge your snack based on their five senses. Would they choose to eat your snack if it was in a store? Ask your testers to give feedback on what could be better. Modify your recipe and try again.

Reflect and Share

How can you improve your recipe? What would be the best way to package your snack?

Glossary

additives—substances added to something in small amounts

artificial—made by humans; not natural

calories—units that measure energy

convenient—suited to a person's comfort or ease

conveyor belt—a moving strip of fabric, metal, or rubber used to transport objects from one place to another

crave—have a strong desire for something

cues—things that serve as signals or suggestions

curing—preparing something that preserves it for storing

emulsifiers—substances that keep liquids from separating

enhance—to make something better

hull—the outer covering of a seed

innovations—new ideas, methods, or devices

legend—a story coming down from the past whose truth is accepted but cannot be proved

monks—male members of a religious group who promise to stay poor, obey the rules of their group, and not get married

obesity—a state of being very overweight

revolution—a sudden, extreme, or complete change in the way people live

starch—a white substance found in some foods, such as corn and potatoes, and used as a thickener in sauces

Index

CAREER ADVICE
from Smithsonian

Do you want to study snacks?
Here are some tips to get you started.

"Food and history have long been a part of my life. As a child, my summers were not filled with trips to Disney World, but with trips to historic sites such as Gettysburg. Find ways to explore your interests. Learning about history helps you find ways to improve inventions of the past."
—*Ashley R. Young, Ph.D., Historian*

"Part of my job is to find objects that should be added to the museum. It's important to record the history of food for future generations. Understanding the science and history of food is important if you want to do this work."
—*Paula Johnson, Museum Curator*